J.D. Calvert

TABLE OF CONTENTS

Aerospace Softball 47

by

J.D. Calvert

ACRONYM LIST

I have tried to keep the number of acronyms used herein to an absolute minimum, but acronyms are an inescapable part of aerospace literature, and so I have necessarily included the ones explained here.

A.S.S. Air-to-Surface Seeker
This is WAC's latest project, a sophisticated missile that is guided by an imaging infrared sensor. The heart of this sensor is its focal plane array of infrared detectors. These need a lot more development, but so far, even with the present FPAs, this missile has successfully sought the surface every time it was launched from the air!

BAC   Bad Aerospace Corporation
This is the competition, and I would accuse them of being ogres and sex deviates if so many of them weren't us and vice versa; that is, there is a lot of transient labor in the aerospace industry. One thing for sure is that when (all too often) BAC beats us out of a big contract it is because they have somehow cheated! We spend a lot of time trying to figure out their secrets of success.

FPA   Focal Plane Array
This is a little tiny chip containing thousands of itsy-bitsy detector elements. On a good day (or night) these detectors can turn a rain of millions of infrared photons into a corresponding stream of electrons which spray out (eventually) onto a television screen and produce a very expensive picture.

I^2R Imaging Infrared or FLIR
Like television but sees in the dark.   Usually the only program you can get is some clown drinking coffee and leaving his warm hand print on his pants.   If you're lucky he may also light a match.

MTF   Modulation Transfer Function
A measure of how well an imaging sensor sees little details in the dark -- like does the clown have his fly zipped.

MCT   merc cad telluride   mercury-cadmium-telluride
This is the primary material used to manufacture FPAs.   If you can discover a vein of this stuff in your mine, you might become a very rich prospector.

MAD   Mission Analysis Department
This group contemplates the military's long term requirements and tries to get WAC into position to bid on big contracts. Their primary tool is the dart board at various Officers Clubs.

SOBAD   Second Order Ballistic Aiming Device
For a couple of years, this sophisticated electronic unit was the big money product for WAC's sister division. Then somebody pointed out that the troops really didn't have much use for an aiming device -- however clever -- when they tossed their hand grenades, and next thing we knew the darn program got cancelled!   (But not before there was a lot of nasty press.)

WAC Wonderful Aerospace Corporation
Somebody has to wear the white hats, and in the aerospace industry WAC got the job. WAC is wonderfully organized: at the top of the heap, so to speak, are engineers-turned-bean-counters and at the bottom is an unruly mob of technical-types who are never happy with any of the decisions handed down to them and couldn't care less about the beans.

INTRODUCTION

This book is a subset collection of smart-ass poems derived from my earlier book
AEROSPACE SOFTBALL*.   Although AEROSPACE SOFTBALL was wildly
successful – three copies sold and 60 Author Copies given away (many mailed) at
some Author Expense – there was feedback to the effect that "I can't stomach
reading this whole damn book cover- to-cover.   Please publish a shorter version
with just the Grade A and Grade B poems !?!"
    *AEROSPACE SOFTBALL, copyright 2020 by J.D. Calvert, Amazon.com

So here it is, starting with this Cover Letter I composed to accompany the 60
Author Copies:

                                                                    3-30-21

 Speaking of annoying, this is a copy of my smart-ass poetry collection,
 Aerospace Softball, whether you need it or not!?!
 (Shut up: Second Prize is TWO copies!?!)

Trust me, even if you never open this book it will look fascinating lying on your
coffee table -- giving your visitors the impression that you _reek_ of kulchur --
OR if you tear out the right number of pages this book will make an excellent
wedge beneath a wobbly coffee table!
                    ****

        To: Amanda Gorman, Poet Laureate of the United States
        From: J.D. Calvert

        Your words are all about
              raising poetry to the level of Art.

        My poetry is all about
              finding words that rhyme with "fart" !?!

3

BACKGROUND

In 1984 the Wonderful Aerospace Corporation (acronym WAC) reinstated a softball program.   On the good side, the game was now co-ed: at least two ladies had to be on the field at all times.   On the bad side (for my money) the game had become "slow pitch": To be declared a *strike* the ball had to be lobbed in an arc that peaked between 6 and 12 feet and then descend to actually strike the rubber of home plate.   Short sighted umpires must have thought this one up!?!

Of course no one asked me for my opinion, what with my legendary athletic skills, but I was nonetheless invited to join our Department slow-pitch softball team.   About half of the team's members were young men who could accurately be described as jocks, but the other half of us were more than able to overcome this handicap.   As my teammate, Wiley, observed: "Most of the players on this team think softball is a venereal disease!"

In addition to selecting our own nickname (emblazoned on our jersey) we democratically chose a team name (I voted for *Master Batters*) and became

As the season unfolded it became apparent the Mad Batters were not going to lead the league, and somehow we lost every game in the regular season – which somehow inspired me to generate a "poem" to our efforts … and then another … and another…

MAD BATTERS '84, BAD ATTITUDES 0

I think we peaked too early
-- we beat the Loggers in the quals --
'Cause from then on it was all downhill
-- in fact it was over the falls !

Tho' the Mad Batters were originated by our Departement Supervisor (he chose the nickname "Bones" for reasons no one ever understood), Bones tricked the newest hire John ("JC") into taking the reins that first disasterous year, and in turn John tricked yours truly into taking the reins for the next many seasons!?!   Did I mention legendary athletic skills? In my new, more responsible – albeit no more knowledgeable – role as Team Captain I followed JC's lead and adopted the newsletter format to publish vital team information -- and the occasional poem – primarily to explain how a seeming loss was in fact another brilliant victory for the Mad Batters!?!

TEAM CAPTAIN'S ESSAY ON PERSPECTIVE
(for MAD BATTER eyes only!?!)

1. The goal is for everyone to play and have fun.

2. Winning is nice but not worth killing for or getting hurt.

3. Playing on this team will NOT lead to a contract
     in professional slow-pitch softball.

4. In this league there are a lot of errors: DO YOUR PART !!

5. As a result of #4 above: If in doubt -- GO FOR IT !!
     -- Hitting, running bases, throwing, catching, drinking!

6. Other key features of Mad Batter style softball:

     o A proper slide into first base can turn even the wimpiest hit
          into an easy single.

     o No ball is hit so high over your head that you can't reach it
          by throwing your glove.

     o Don't get discouraged if the enemy team seems to be pulling ahead
          -- they're also getting tired faster.

     o Proper execution of the Mad Batter Shuffle
          can turn even the best enemy offense into mush!

     o There is never any doubt when it comes time to decide
          whether to play one more inning
               or to head for Post Game Attitude Adjustment.

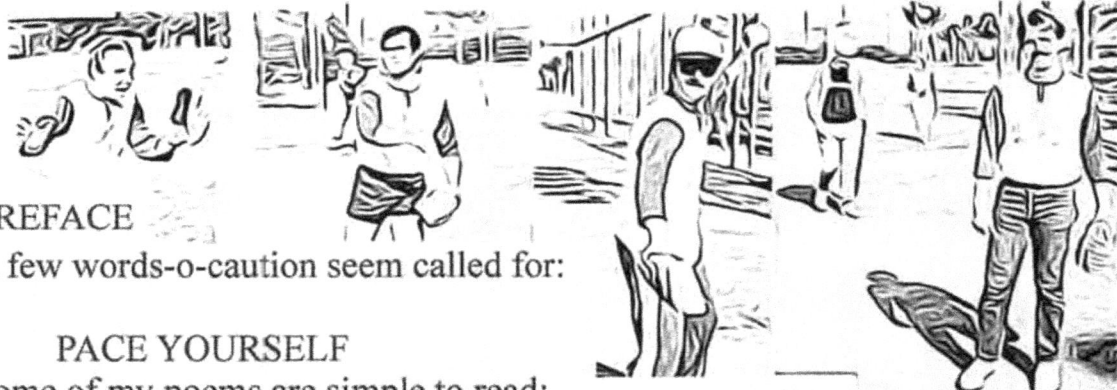

PREFACE
A few words-o-caution seem called for:

PACE YOURSELF
Some of my poems are simple to read:
The beat is smooth and lazy.
Many of the others
 require quite a bit of effort:
finding the rhythm just makes you crazy!?!

AND / OR

I've polished this poetry over and over
-- it's driving me 'round the bend ! --
Alas there are so many syllables to consider
that I fear it will / wonder will it / never end !?!

MERRY CHRISTMAS TO THE MADRIGALS OF '84

Here's to the magic Madrigal Singers of Edison High School:
    Your singing is *fantastic*, and your looks are really cool.
        A lot of your success, of course, is also Mr. Otey's;
        I think the guy could get harmony
            from a pack of wild coyotes!
And when you're not on stage you throw
    a party that's really great;
        I only hope you don't get a lot of gas
            from the ton of food you ate.
You'll always look back proudly
    on these years when your voices grew.
        I wish you continued happiness,
            and may all of your dreams come true!

TO A SPECIAL PERSON IN THE CHOIR

Your voice is weak and whiny,
    you hardly ever know your part,
        And when we sing *pianissimo*
            everyone can hear you fart!

UP, UP AND AWAY

Once upon a time there was a ball team
        with a very tall Mad Batter;
                Sadly for us all next year
                        we'll have the former but not the latter.
'Cause Art's leaving WAC to try out
        BAC's swamp in Seal Beach,
                And tho' we'll miss him here,
                        we wish him well
                                in his search for new heights to reach.
But what about poor Harold:
        now who can he look up to?
                And who'll be there when we need someone
                        to chug a pitcher of beer or two?
Grow up Art; your leaving
        is really shortsighted and bad!
                How can you give up on a company
                        that makes a product line called SOBAD?
And it's more than a little tacky to split
        right after winning the contest First Prize
                For a smart-ass cheeky caption
                        (attached right here before your eyes).
But then again as I recall,
        he greeted the prize with mixed emotion
                -- Something about hangovers combined with catamarans
                        and trips upon the ocean.
So here's to Art: a helluva nice guy;
        For his quality work he should be paid a bounty.
                Although he'll be gone, you can still spot his shadow:
                        it's the one that spans all of Orange County!

MAKIN' A MOVE ON TUSCON

Steve is on the move again;
    his ass is out the door.
        We'll miss him at the ball games
           and at the parties even more!
But BAC has made him an offer
    to be a part-time professional student,
        And if you can get a deal such as that,
           take it! if you're wise and prudent.
BAC has even assured him
    that he'll still be near the beach ....
        … Never mind the Gila monsters
           and the cattle bones left to bleach.
Never mind as well the girls
    with skin tanned the texture of the bark of trees;
        You wouldn't kiss them anyway
           since 9 out of 10 have herpes.
And while we're listing some negatives,
    don't forget the Apaches are surly;
        They're still pissed off about their land,
           and their favorite scalps are curly.
Of course there are some good things too,
    and I'd list them both if I could,
        But I'm all choked up about his leaving
           so my memory's not too good.
Adios to the guy we've all come to like
    in the short time that we've worked with him;
        To the guy who once couldn't spell SOBAD
           -- and even today his chances seem slim.
Adios to the guy who's decent and kind
    and wears his heart upon his sleeve;
        Who, when asked for a clever nickname
           to put on his Mad Batters jersey,
              without hesitation replied, "Steve" !

FOCAL PLANE ARRAYS AND OTHER SHIT

Some of my earliest "poetry" was aimed (in *fun*, guys, honest!) at the people who design and develop the little electronic chips that detect infrared energy and allow our missiles to "see" in the dark.

This is an uncertain science, depending on dogged persistence to search for just the right chemistry and procedures to produce a reliable detector. There is absolutely no way of predicting, within a decade, when this search will find success, and each new detector design is pretty much a new ballgame, so to speak.

It is a true paradox of aerospace contracting, therefore, that the detector people must not only schedule their minor miracles but also forecast a commensurate cost.   Guess what? They are very often wrong on both counts!

Well, inasmuch as our proposed systems* count on these detectors' performance -- not to mention their existence -- I feel it is my duty to pick on our detector group without mercy! Lucky for me they are a good natured lot -- not counting, that is, the occasional appearance of noxious gases in our building's air conditioning system after the posting of a particularly acrid poem.
  *For example A.S.S. and SOBAD

TIME FOR A DRIBBLE FROM THE PIPELINE?

Greetings to the Ashlyholes from Systems
      -- you know we's really Mean! --
            we'd like delivery of a full FPA
                  by Friday, December 13.
'Though we're well aware that this day
      normally carries an evil curse,
            we figure where FPAs are concerned
                        our luck can't really get any worse !

IT AIN'T OVER 'TIL IT'S OVER

In '82 the message was simple and mean:
     "Good detectors are few and far between."
        Sneakier in '83:
           "What a spectre, All systems GO -- but no detector!"
Upbeat in '84: "A.S.S taking a ride
     with eyes -- Ashlyholes willing -- of merc cad telluride."
       Now here we are in '85,
          Our hopes are dimmer but still alive,
And the Wonderful Aerospace crack detector team
     (Oops! a poor choice of words it would seem)
        Is still closing in with every passing day
          on the elusive and mysterious MCT FPA,
And they never give up,
     and they shrug off every rhyme,
       'Cause their clocks are calibrated
         in units of geological time !

THE LABS ARE EMPTY BUT THE CONFERENCE ROOMS ARE FULL

     Given that good detectors
        are few and far between
          And that there are many, many
            detector secrets left to glean
    And given that it's impossible
       to schedule a technology breakthru
         And that WAC's staff
           of detector technologists is few
   Then how can it be
      -- by what management quirk --
        That this staff spends more time
         at status meetings
           than they do at work?!?

THE *I AIN'T GOT NO DETECTOR* BLUES ... REPRISE

Imagine this--what a spectre -- all systems Go but no detector!
    A crime you say?... Depends on your perspective of course:
        Could it be instead
            some planner got the cart before the horse?

After all, Jim always cautioned
    that our plans might be wildly optimistic,
        And that what we had scheduled had never been done before
           so there was no knowing what was realistic.

But he was always so *cheerful* when he said it
    that we thought he might be kidding,
        And when we asked him for the best imaginable FPA
           we forgot to ask if that went
              with the cost and schedule we were bidding.

Well, the system we envisioned was so fantastic -- had it only worked --
    it would've made national headlines.
        If only those darn detector folks
           had met our randomly chosen deadlines.

And having missed our arbitrary milestone dates
    you think they'd all be tearful,
        But when we looked in the laboratory windows
           Jim and the gang
             always seemed so depressingly *cheerful !?!*

As though they were satisfied doing the best job they could,
    making progress steadily, bit by bit;
        As though -- you don't suppose!?! --
           they always knew our schedules and costs
             were just a lot of bullshit!!!

OUTTA HERE

Here's to the A.S.S.holes: the seeker's finally out the door!
So, in a nostalgic mood, I re-read the proposal
written many years before.

It now appears we may have been optimistic
-- do the adverb "wildly" ring a bell? --
Especially the part about "Low-Cost, Low-Risk Approach"
and about "a High Confidence Schedule" as well.

On the other hand, WAC's the one who predicted
"Good Detectors are Few and Far Between,"
And we've certainly demonstrated *that* to be a fact
so please don't treat us mean!

Besides, the progress and learning
have been substantial in every technical respect,
And you *can* see a long wavelength infrared image
even though the quality is not up to spec.

Furthermore our seeker is software programmable
-- everybody knows that's modern and good --
I just wish it didn't require three full-time programmers
to generate a picture that looks like it should.

So how to respond to A.S.S. critics who point out
ADO's been dissolved and MICOM is broke?
Say, "Picky, picky, picky" for one thing
and then, "Screw 'em if they can't take a Joke!"

I TOLD YOU SO

Here's to the inquisitors of A.S.S.
They're out to decipher this incredible mess.
It'll be complicated,
but their result can be anticipated:
Of cartoons and rhymes there should be more
and of technical specs there should be less !!

THE TUESDAY AFTER

Okay, so we lost one critical game to an arch rival – result: MAD BATTERS 8, GOING DOWN AGAIN 18.   Don't forget, they're all getting older faster than we are!?!

Absolutely brilliant pitching for a last place C-3 team!   When you consider that Going Down Again is world renown for their patience in waiting for a walk, our pitching staff didn'r really do too bad – I know we didn't walk in 18 runs!   Attaboys Ralph and Wiley II too!   I would also like to point out that these guys don't just pitch, they are part of our C-3 class infield defense as well, moving to cover and/or backup weak spots.   Ralph, for example, made a sensational tag at home plate – saving the assigned catcher (your Team Captain) from a(nother) debacle.   The video unit did a marvelous job of capturing John's unbelievable double play in the 6th inning – snaring Sid's long flyball to left and then nailing Jim going back to first base!?!   Come the war I'm giving all my hand grenades to John!!

The rest of the defense performed damn good too, and if I had connected to Bones on a couple of easy pickoffs, and if that tall guy hadn't hit those home runs, and if there hadn't been quite as many errors, I'm sure this would have been an entirely different ballgame!?!

But however well our defense might have performed, our offense could have been even better!   Alas our hits were too few and too far between and not very far in the middle either where most of them were caught by Ollie and thrown to Leo before we got to first base.

Luckily there were essentially no fans in attendance to verify our performance, and I have the only copy of the video.   Trust me team, when the image processing is finished we're gonna do okay!?!

Post Game Attitude Adjustment was interesting because both the Mules (our next victims) and Found On Road Dead (the following week) had K.O.ed their enemies by mercy rule; boy have we made these two teams overconfident or what!?!   I can hardly wait!   Of course Captain Kurt didn't have the faintest idea that it was us he played next, so he's probably out right now recruiting ringers like crazy.   No matter Kurt, this one is ours! And Roach, you're next !!

HO HUM. MARK MAKES ANOTHER CATCH.

MAD BATTER DATA FOR VIDEO UNIT

Players in nominal batting order; batting average to date and nominal defensive position listed in parens after each name. All data guaranteed to be at least somewhat truthful and accurate; no sexual harassment intended no matter how sexy the person is!

COACH JOHN (.667, center field).   John is the team coach so any bad play executions by any Mad Batter are his fault. John is also to blame for taking over the team in its infancy during the first season (after Bones had dumped us). John proceeded to shape the team into a precision slow-pitch softball machine, and we had a perfect regular season that first year except for winning our playoff game.

CHRIS (.500, 3rd base). Chris is having an excellent year except she tends to stop a lot of hits to third base with her body; next year we're thinking of teaching her what the glove is for.

BRAD (.743, shortstop). Brad's having slightly more than a fair year: 10 HRs and 36 RBIs so far. Nonetheless his personal coach, Wiley, says there are still tricks that Brad needs to learn; since I am sworn to avoid sexual harassment, you'll have to ask Wiley yourself.

LINDA (.429, 2nd base or rover). Linda joined the Mad Batters after the season began, to fill in for Bob who -- as you well know -- left us unexpectedly. What a good deal that has turned out to be: not only has she played better softball than Bob ever did, but also (since she works in HR on the 4th floor of the Admin building) now we can get the passes to Disneyland without waiting for the damn elevator!

MARK (.656, left field). Mark has had another excellent year, although he is newly married (December), and this seems to be sapping some of his energy (surprise!). Mark's specialty is finding potholes in left field while making sensational running catches. The team vet is saving a bullet with Mark's name on it.

RUSS (.480, right field). Why they nicknamed him "Shuffle" is a mystery to me; Russ is so fast that if the bases were laid out in a straight line (the way they should be for C-3 League where backup is everything!) he'd have already scored a run before you could even say FO!! And that's not all.

DAVE { BONES } (.515, first base). Bones originated the Mad Batters for the '84 season but soon suckered John into taking over. Worse yet, Bones stayed on to "help" the team by playing first base -- just kidding, Dave!   Bones is also the team base-running coach and simultaneously serves as the Official Mad Batter Statue.

JUDY (.125, 2nd base or rover). For an interesting variety of reasons, Judy played with us in the pre-season games but missed the entire first half of the regular season.   And for reasons not yet clear, the team has been doing about as well now as it did before she rejoined us; if anyone can find meaning in this, I am sure it is our crack video unit?

JERRY (.478, center & rover). Jerry injured himself in our last game and may not be playing tonight. It is ironic that Jerry hurt himself in the *leg* going after a flyball because everyone on the team was betting he would be injured in one of his other bodily protrusions; you have to watch Jerry's catching style to appreciate this.

JACK DAVID (.519, third or fourth). This is *The Mouth's* 2nd year as the Mad Batters' Team Captain (not to be confused with Coach; see John above). Any decent plays executed by the Mad Batters are the direct result of the Team Captain's inspirational leadership. In some desperation, he's been played at right field lately where he has become a *triple* threat: not only can't he catch, but also he can share his thoughts (?) with both our own and the adjacent diamond.

RALPH (.444, pitcher). Ralph won the Sue-Look-Alike contest (judges were blindfolded to eliminate any chance of discrimination) and became our pitcher this year. He is doing a sensational job, I don't care what they say! He has pitched every game except one, has been in trouble with almost every batter, and yet we are in next-to-last place within C-3 League. So clearly Ralph still has a lot of potential left. And furthermore, no pitcher in all of slow-pitch softball is more cool on the mound: penguins would shit at his feet if available to do so. (I don't have time to fix every typo.)

WILEY (.400, catcher, 2nd base). If you think you see Wiley at this game, you need to clean the lens of your camera because he is on an extended vacation helping major league baseball teams get back on track (like the *Senators*, for example). Wiley has played an absolutely sensational game this year (relative to last year) and is eyeing Bones' baserunner coaching job for next year.

JUNE (.333, catcher, 2nd base). June has fielded more fans (3) for one game than any other Mad Batter so far this year. She has also become a C-3 class catcher including a pre-season tag of Big Bill sliding into home and several near misses in the regular season. Furthermore her bat has been responsible for more than 75% of our hits this season (but it needs new tape on the handle, June).

JILL (.200, catcher, 2nd base). Jill has improved dramatically this year. She was crippled for part of the season with knee injuries and bridal showers, but she is 100% for today's game, and we need her enthusiasm to carry us past the low points: for example when it looks like we might Mercy Rule the enemy team, she'll say something like, "I doubt it!", and so far she has always been right.

HENRY { SHOE } (.478, 2nd base). Nicknamed "the late Henry" by Wiley, Henry has never been on time for a game that anyone can remember, but now that he's near the end of the batting order there's a chance he can take his turn. Henry played third base early in the season until it was discovered that Chris has a better arm among other things.

KATHY (.000, ready reserve). Kathy signed on as ready reserve for the team in case we ran short of the required 2 ladies necessary for a game. So far she was called on once and played a very credible game (for the wife of our coach). Her batting average of .000 is after only 2 trips to the plate and thus by Mad Batter standards is no measure of her potential -- we sincerely hope!

The Mad Batters + Mule & the Gang

MULE & THE GANG DATA FOR VIDEO UNIT

Names listed in random order; no telling how they'll bat or even who will show up for the game. Batting average and nominal defensive position are in parens after each name. All data is true to the best of anyone's knowledge, since this team has no written records.

DOUG (.125, 2nd base). Doug joined the Mules after about one-third of the season was over, when his passion for rescuing helpless animals overcame his better judgment one evening at *Chester Drawers*.

BYRON (.125, shortstop). Byron is the shy guy on this team, but he is beginning to respond to post game shyness therapy at *Chester Drawers*.

{ WILD } BILL (.125, 3rd base). When Bill was asked if he knew anything at all about softball, he said, "No, but I'm a party animal!" Kurt understood Bill to say he was "partly animal" and added him to the Mule's roster immediately.

KATHLEEN (.478, catcher). Kathleen is the only good ball player on this team, so with typical strategic brilliance Kurt has her playing catcher.

KURT (.125, right field). Kurt is captain of the Mules. He explains his role by saying, "If the shoe fits, wear it!", and then hee-haws like a jackass. It fits, Kurt!

LOU (.125, center field). Last year, playing 3rd base, Lou became the only player in WAC softball history to execute a triple play (ironically against the Mad Batters). Unfortunately, nobody on either team realized what had happened, and Kurt has moved Lou to center field until he stops whimpering about it.

TERRI (.573, rover). Two years ago Terri played for a professional women's softball team, but they missed the National Championship by one game. Totally dejected, she married Robert and is now carrying out her promise to get as far from professional-quality softball as possible.

ROBERT (.125, left field). Despite shock therapy (cleverly administered at work via bad designs he is asked to test), Robert still bats backwards, but at least they have convinced him to stand on the wrong side of the plate to compensate.

KEN (.125, first base). Ken wields a mean bat at times, but in the long run his average seems about the same as the other Mules. Ken's defensive specialties are staining his official Mule tee-shirt with sweat and trying not to look frustrated about all the bad throws to first base.

JOE { JAYVEE } (.995, pitcher). After helping to start this team last year, Joe suckered Kurt into being the captain; now Joe just pitches and keeps the team stats .... to himself !?!

SNATCHING POETRY FROM THE JAWS OF DEFEAT

The last half of inning seven
    was the last chance the Mad Batters had;
        The Mules were up by four whole runs,
           but the Batters wanted this one bad.
Well, Brad's drive went right thru Bill at third,
    who saw Brad go to second and swore.
        Then Linda hit to JayVee the pitcher;
           throwing her out at first allowed Brad to score.
So now the gap was only three,
    and Russ stood ready at the plate;
        He hit a shot to Teri the rover,
           but with his speed
              the throw to first was too late.
Next Mark moved strongly up to bat,
    his reputation making him seem ten feet tall,
        And the Mules' eyes grew round
           (and several wet their garish pants)
              'cause they knew he could really pound that ball !
And pound it he did, on the very first pitch,
    but alas the wind took it foul;
        And double alas, his next long drive was caught --
           now the Mules let out their jackass howl !
Bones kept it alive with a single, however,
    advancing Russ to second base,
        And JayVee fell apart at the seams, so to speak,
           walking Judy and getting egg on his face.
Thus the bases were loaded and two were out
    as Team Captain took his strange batting stance.
        The video unit announced, "Team goat's at the plate;
           the Mad Batters haven't a chance!"
Now it's true that he was 0 for 2 on the day,
    still the odds were even he might give it a smash;
        So the air was electric as he foul-tipped strike two,
           and when the next three were balls
              you could feel lightning flash !

At the pitcher's mound JayVee was bathed in sweat,
    and the crowd's roar drowned out by his pounding heart;
        While at the plate the umpire turned his head in disgust
            as Captain expressed *his* tension with an enormous fart.
JayVee's arm swooped thru an arc and released the ball
    -- not a heart dared beat in any chest --
        And even the flies that surround every Mule
            remained motionless as the ball's trajectory reached its crest.
Down it began, picking up speed;
    watching the seams you could see it slowly turn.
        Everyone could tell that it was going to be close,
            and now every stomach began to churn.
Thru the glare off his nose
    Team Captain watched the ball descend,
        and all three muscles in his body were tense.
He knew that a Grand Slam
    was what his team needed from him now,
        preferably a clean one,
            clear over the damn fence !
And he mused on how
    he'd then be carried off on the team's shoulders
        -- as it turned out that was somewhat his fate --
For just as in his reveries
    he started a modest speech with, "It was nothing..."
        from the corner of his eye
            he saw the ball bounce on the plate!
Crawling away, the Captain was surrounded by Mules
    and hoisted up
        for a victory lap around the track.
Still standing on first,
    Judy hollered after in frustration,
        "Keep him you Asses;
            we don't want him back!"
Everywhere at beaches in Southern California
    happy people are surfing and getting a tan,
        But there's no joy among Mad Batters
            -- nor much surprise either --
                'cause their Team Captain has screwed up again!?!

WHOA! ROAD APPLES ON THE TRAIL
Here's to the Mules: each and every one an Ass,
And worse, nary *one* with even a little bit of class;
But I admit their reflexes are fast
'Cause when I buy a pitcher to replace the last
They're always the first ones there holding out an empty glass !!!

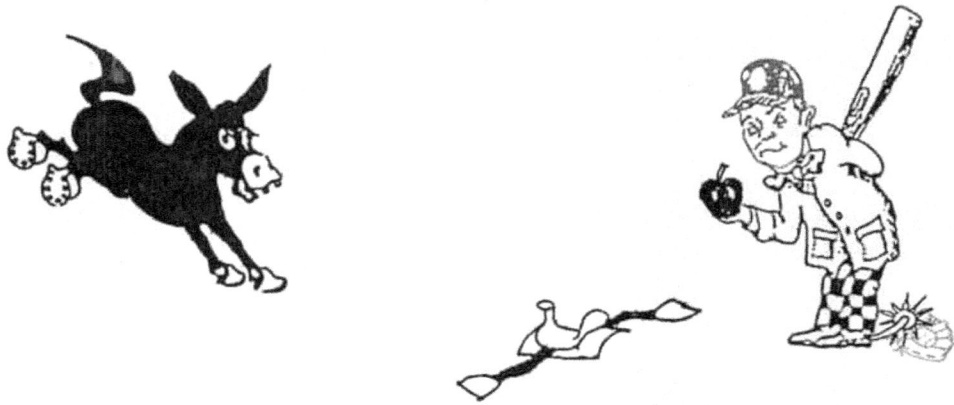

WELCOME TO C-3 LEAGUE
Once there was a ball team called "Found On Road Dead";
By a "dain bramaged" captain called "Roach" they were led.
Their roster'd split your sides because
A funnier collection of names never was –
No wonder they Adjust Attitudes all night instead of going to bed !?!

MAD BATTERS '86, BAD ATTITUDES 0

Here's to the Mad Batters -- again -- it was another fantastic season!
You're not just another fun softball team, you're special!
... give me a minute and I'll think of a reason.
Not "special" like "Special Olympics" (although at times it's hard to tell)
But "special" like super nice people
who just don't happen to play softball very well.
Who nonetheless try their hardest to have fun in every game;
Who play every game as though it were our first,
but play to win, no matter how lame.
Whose legendary slides into first base
have never resulted in injuries requiring the team vet
('Tho in truth your best slides've been into the bench,
just in time to avoid a forfeit).
Who retire to Post Game Attitude Adjustment to celebrate
-- no matter we win, lose or draw --
And who do so with such decorum and class
that even the Mules are in awe!
Who adjust their attitudes so enthusiastically
before they stroll out *Chester Drawers*' door,
that most of Friday morning is spent in the head
reading the newsletter to learn what happened the day before.
So here's to the Mad Batters: it's been 3 seasons;
Time really does fly when you're having a good time!
Thank you all very much !!
(And yes, I know it seems like hours now
your Team Captain's been reading this stupid rhyme !)

YOU'RE OKAY IF I'M UPWIND

Here's to Mule & the Gang:
a herd of jackasses and proud of it too! ?!
And before every game (to establish their "rep")
they all stomp their feet in donkey "doo",
And then for good measure
-- its disgusting but true --
they rub some in their hair;
Well needless to say there's no mistaking this team
for they have an unmistakable air!
As if their style of softball wasn't enough!
'cause they play like a bunch of asses,
And would have scored nary a single run
had not opposing defenses fled upwind
while their baserunner passes !!

23

MAD ABOUT THIS CHRISTMAS PARTY

Christmas Cheers to the MAD group
    (even the ones with a funny sounding name):
        Without your global insights
            our proposals just wouldn't be the same.
On the other hand, now that I think about it,
    I'm not sure exactly what MADness you really do,
        Although I know it's global and that
            our proposals just wouldn't be the same without you!
I'm really glad to be here
    and to share your eats and drinks
        -- I'm sure your insights are global
            no matter what everyone else thinks!
But never mind the details
    'cause this party is really classy.
        (I just wish Bob's secret bean dip recipe
            hadn't made me get so gassy.)
Of course we'll eat and drink and sing
    and have a really merry time,
        And then we'll suffer in silent misery
            while we read this stupid rhyme.
And we'll keep our hands to ourselves
    lest we be charged with sexual harassment
        (Although they're having a lot more fun
            at the SOBAD party where the perverts went.)
We're glad to be together
    at this special time of year;
        Our teamwork and our friendships
            are what make life seem so dear.
We'd like to think our work's been good
    and made the Nation's enemies a lot more cautious.
        So Merry Christmas and Happy New Year
            (I've got to stop now --
                this poem's starting to make me nauseous!)

RED TEAM BLUES

Monday I was assigned to a Red Team
    and given one of our proposals to review.
        I finished the job just last night,
            and now I'm feeling blue!
First I read the customer's requirements;
    then I read what we'd proposed.
        You guessed it: there was scant correlation!
            ... an entire pad of Deficiencies I composed!!
It wasn't even clear to me
    that I had read the right proposal,
        And I wasn't sure whether to just laugh at the Joke
            or take it straight to the garbage disposal.
The themes tended to be shallow and asinine,
    like "We have the right design!" and "It's the best!"
        And the technical stuff was truly amazing:
            "Our design weighs 200 pounds but is small enough
                to be carried in the soldier's vest!"
Another among my "favorite" lines
    was where "Heisenberg was uncertain, but we're not!"
        And "Now that our entire staff is upgrading the test set,
            our detector's sensitivity has improved quite a lot."
The good news is: there were plenty of graphics,
    'tho what they meant was a mystery to me.
        Half of them were packed with unlabeled data,
            and the other half too small to see.
I read the proposal carefully,
    and I tried not to judge too quick,
        But by the time I had finished the Introduction & Summary
            I was already unbelievably sick.
I continued reading into the System Description
    -- now I wish I had been more cautious --
        'cause when I finished Section 2.1
            my mouth was dry and I was feeling nauseous.
Even so I proceeded forward
    -- relatively speaking I liked 2.2 a whole bunch --
        Alas, Section 2.3 was one step too far:
            I ran to the head and barfed my lunch!
Well needless to say, I used up many red pens;
    when I was thru the sight wasn't pretty!
        But I managed to sum it up
            in a single Principle Comment: "This proposal is totally shitty!"

ALAS POOR YORK; I KNEW HIM WELL

Here's to the Rescuees:
    We're glad to have you aboard.
        We're sorry that your program sank --
           albeit corporate profits have soared!
So don't think of yourselves as failures
    'cause your personal loss has become the company's gain,
        And we'll be glad to take over your building
           'cause this one leaks when it begins to rain …
Of course there'll be some adjustments:
    You'll be a "C-maggot" or "A.S.S.hole" instead of a "Big Gun",
        And you'll have to adapt to schizophrenic air conditioning
           In a building where you never see the sun;
But other than that it's wonderful
    And there's certainly work aplenty,
        And you can begin to relax and not worry about hiding
           From the cameras of 20/20 !?!

Some of my poems dealt with more profound issues than others .....

NO SHIT

How many person-hours are wasted in the head
    When they could be spent enhancing
        our product's performance instead?

Of course I realize that we all generate
    a certain amount of bodily waste,
        And I'm not suggesting we fool with Mother Nature
           and attempt these functions with undue-haste.

Indeed, at *that* end of our head call
    the problem doesn't exist;
        Nay, instead -- and believe me
        this really has me pissed! --

It's after you've heeded nature's call
    that needless time begins to burn,
        While you struggle with
           what ought to be the simplest aerospace problem:
             making the roll of toilet paper turn !!

VERSE 2: A CLASS ACT

Here's to the head of facilities
    (I hope you don't think this too crass)
        Thanks for resolving the toilet paper problem:
        A shitty job but handled with class !!

SOUND EFFECTS

In the earliest days of electronic voice technology the available
"vocabulary" was extremely limited, and -- at Dori's request --
I managed to generate the following ditty within those limits.

    HIGH -- THIS IS DIGITALKER
        READY TWO GO
    FOUR A GREAT TIME
        TRY ONE DOLLAR
           IN THE SPACE BELOW
    FOUR A GREATER TIME
        PLUS S-E-X
           TRY A MILLION DOLLARS --
             PLEASE NO CHECKS !?!

THE MONDAY AFTER

Well wasn't that special!?! Except for another bad data point (8 runs) in the second inning we woulda' had 'em! However the official score was ETA PIZZA PI 13, MAD BATTERS 9 after 7 long innings of struggle. At the half-way point of the season, guess which team is in last place gang? Anyway it was another fun game on the path to nowhere in particular.

Sideline activity verged on chaos. Chris & Bart brought this monster animal of some kind who variously dragged Ralph's kids and/or the backstop around in pursuit of one of our softballs – hereafter known as "the slimy one" – while Katie busied herself demonstrating that personal energy goes in inverse proportion to some power of the age-mass product. As a direct consequence I'm pretty sure the Pi's 8-run inning was the result of a severely distracted umpire!?!

Post Game Attitude Adjustment was a fantastic almost-victory party since the Mules and F.O.R.D. had joined us in "close games". To my delight, Freight Train had to leave early, and after the Mule's late shift (Jane & Jeannie) left, soul survivors Captain Kurt and your Team Captain dug in and prepared to outlast F.O.R.D. …. It soon became clear, however, that Roach and the Tesdall sisters were actually getting their second wind – Steve was just breaking wind, but it did give him more room on the dance floor. After an in-depth discussion of what perverse power the age-mass product should be raised to (Karen's guess: "You're both shitheads !") we gave up and left.

TALK TO YOUR CAPTAIN

Q. You have been muttering inanely about "In-the-park home runs". Talk is cheap – especially in your case – can you be more specific for once?!?

A. Thank you for your diplomatically phrased question, Brad. As a matter of fact I do have a plan for easy Mad Batter style in-the-park home runs: Consider that the weakest spots in any C-3 League defense are the catcher, right field and second base; third base is marginal (hold your thoughts, Brad). Thus to get an easy in-the-park home run all you have to do is get a fairly wimpy hit over the third baseperson's head. Then you <u>just keep running</u> until you get back to home plate ! Wasn't that easy?!? Meanwhile, the third baseperson will have dropped back to get the ball, narrowly avoiding a collision with the left fielder, rover and shortstop. Noticing that you have rounded first and are on your way to second, the third baseperson will make a terrible throw to the second baseperson who will make a fascinating attempt to catch the ball which will thus go on out into right field. Their shortstop – always the best player on the team (now don't you feel terrible, Brad) – will watch all this with total disgust; CAUTION: he/she may try to trip you as you go by – you know how short-tempered shortstops are ! The right field person will have no trouble picking up the overthrow from second because the ball will have rolled to a complete stop before he/she gets to it – although there will be some confusion because the center fielder, shortstop – they're quick – first and second basepersons and the pitcher will narrowly avoid colliding in the scramble. By the time the ball is fielded you will be around third and on your way to home. Guess what? They will still try to throw you out at home! So now it is you versus their catcher who will not only have you and the ball coming in hard, but also their entire defense will be converging on the plate en masse in a desperate effort to help the catcher; guess what that does to the catcher's concentration on the ball?!? Don't even *think* about sliding; go in standing up!

IT'S ONLY A(NOTHER) GAME

Ugly rumors notwithstanding,
     the players of Haagen-Dazs
          (With a couple of notable exceptions)
               apparently don't wear bras.
On the other hand, it seems to me
     those suckers can really bat
          And kept our crack defensive unit
               chasing this hit and that.
So despite outstanding efforts,
     we seem to have lost again;
          Tho' after innings one and two
               I thought we might actually win!
A bunch of the Mad Batters
     hit real or near home runs,
          And June got hits and an RBI
               -- no kidding! Bless her buns!
Mark's pitching blazed, and of
     his plate coverage no one could scoff;
          Laura really hustled,
               and u-no-who yelled his A.S.S. off.
So we were definitely on our game
     and played exceptionally great;
          It's just that winning this one
               was not to be our fate.
But what the hell, we're six and oh*;
     Way to go Team!
          Let's keep up this momentum
               and this incredible head of steam!
If we can roll on thru the playoffs
     and make it thru this year,
          We'll have spent more time than anyone
               crying in our beer!

---

*Well okay, it's really 0 and 6, but that version is depressing, and besides it doesn't rhyme!

HEY, LIGHTEN UP; IT'S NOT HAPPENING TO ME

Here's to Don and Betty Trailar
    and a marriage of an incredible sort:
        Incredibly fun, incredibly romantic,
            And – given divorce statistics – probably incredibly short.
And speaking of short, Don, here's some honeymoon advice:
    Don't rush sticking your Trailar "tongue"
        into Betty's Trailar "hitch";
            First warm up her motor and lubricate all the parts
                or you may learn the meaning
                    of the cliché "Life's a bitch !"
Meanwhile, Betty, be patient and understanding;
    Don's nice, but he's not too bright;
        His head's still full of all that macho shit;
            you'll have to use cunning to train him right.
And both be aware that marital bliss is accompanied by problems,
    like sharing the bathroom
        and arguing over every decision you make.
            You'll both have to make sacrifices and surrender half your freedom
                …Are you sure marriage isn't a big mistake?
Well never mind now; go forward you lovebirds;
    share the good times and the bad times come what may.
        I'm really sincerely glad you're getting married
            because I never liked either of you anyway!
But seriously folks, I'm happy for Don and Betty
    and think they're really first rate.
        May your union last forever and your dreams all be fuilfulled;
            May good health and happiness be your fate !!

And I was never invited to give another wedding toast ever again !??!

WHAT'S A NICE KID LIKE YOU...?

Congratulations to Bob and Valerie,
     and Happy Birthday to Francis Shelby !
          The miracle of birth is now behind
              -- and speaking of history --
                    your carefree days might as well be!
Because now the contest really begins:
     parenting's a mixture of pleasure and pain,
          and it's not going to be easy for daughter Shelby either
              what with you two being so hard to train.
But lucky for baby, her crying's tuned to the frequency
     that makes Mom and Dad's life a living hell;
          So within a couple of months
              you'll be giving her not only what she needs
                  but everything she *wants* as well.
Good news: at that point it begins to be fun;
     watching a child learn and develop's a joy to be seen;
          And it's important to stock up on all these wonderful memories
              -- you'll need to fall back on them when she becomes a teen!
Meanwhile we're all very happy for you three
     and for all the love that you share for each other
          ... But don't get carried away (albeit none of our business)
           unless you want Shelby to have a baby sister or brother!?!

A SHORT POEM FOR YOUR BIRTHDAY

Here's to Joan:
    the short secretary we all adore.
        (Uses file drawers one, two and three
            as steps for climbing to file drawer four).
A very Happy Birthday Joan;
    Tho' we can all see that you're short,
        If measured in units of Lady-per-Inch,
            you're slam-dunk champ of the court!!

ANOTHER JOAN POEM

Here's to our favorite short lady named Joan.
    Spends her days typing and answering the phone.
        May your birthday be the best
        And the same for all the rest
We'd still like you even if another foot you'd grown !!

    SHORT NOTICE
Here's a poem that's really short:
    HAPPY BIRTHDAY SPORT !

        or

Many people are born in the fall,
    And many people are slender and tall,
        And many people are grouchy and mean
        With a face and disposition too ugly to be seen!
Happy Birthday Joan: you're not like any of those people at all !!!

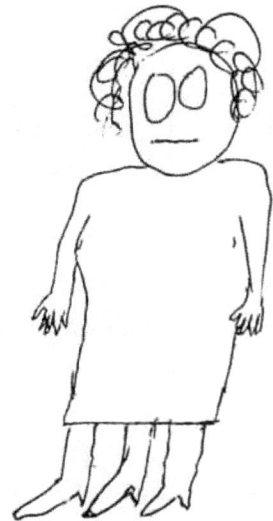

HEY, IT'S ONLY A JOB WELL DONE

Happy Secretary's Day Joan:
    we all think you're absolutely the best!
        And we not only think so on this one short day
            but also on all the rest.
We thank you for all that you do for us all
    -- especially the donuts and the typing so swift --
        And by way of demonstrating that our feelings for you are sincere,
            we all chipped in on this gift.
It cost us the better part of ten dollars,
    and the salesperson said it was quality stuff,
        But no matter how extravagant we went for the present
            we can never ever thank you enough.
Well that about says it; we hope you got the message:
    we think you're a lady of the most incredible sort:
        Incredibly fun, incredibly smart, incredibly nice
        -- and incredibly short !!

SHORT REFRAIN

Re Secretary Days:
    Skip the praise;
        Where's the raise?'.?

ONE MORE TIME …

As the countdown to the end of this '88 season closes rapidly on Zero, the MAD BATTERS have begun to get their act together, fielding a full 10 person team (eventually) to deliver a stunning 26 – 4 victory to POULTRY IN MOTION – but guess which team had the 4? The feathers are still flying after this broiling hot game!?!

At the mound again Ralph used every pitch in his cookbook to hold Hank's paltry flock of poultry to a mere 26 runs in 3.5 blazing innings. Ralph's pitching was significantly enhanced by Chris at third base who devastated the random Poultry batter with an occasional terrorized shriek, "HERE COMES THE COLONEL !!"

Aside from the pitching and verbal abuse, however, our defense mainly depended on John to catch flying Poultry balls to get us out of each inning. Hank definitely had the green light on, and the Mad Batters had a workout chasing hits – not to mention the agony of our one-arm scorekeeper, June, trying to keep track of it all.

Alas, Hank's victory dance was dampened considerably in the last inning when he broke his leg sliding into home plate – why anyone in C-3 League would slide into any base other than First remains a complete mystery to your Team Captain. The team vet was fairly drooling at the prospect of performing surgery on a Poultry and had a little pop-up thermometer all set, but the darn Paramedics elbowed him aside.

NICE SLIDE, HANK....?

Hey Hank, the Mad Batters penned for you this very sweet little poem;
We're all real sorry that you broke your leg sliding into home.
And of course we hope your recovery is swift,
…. 'Cause otherwise we might feel compelled
to chip in for a gift !?!

And here's some really good medical advice
Straight to you from the Mad Batters' team vet:
From now on use your other leg
whenever you pirouette !!

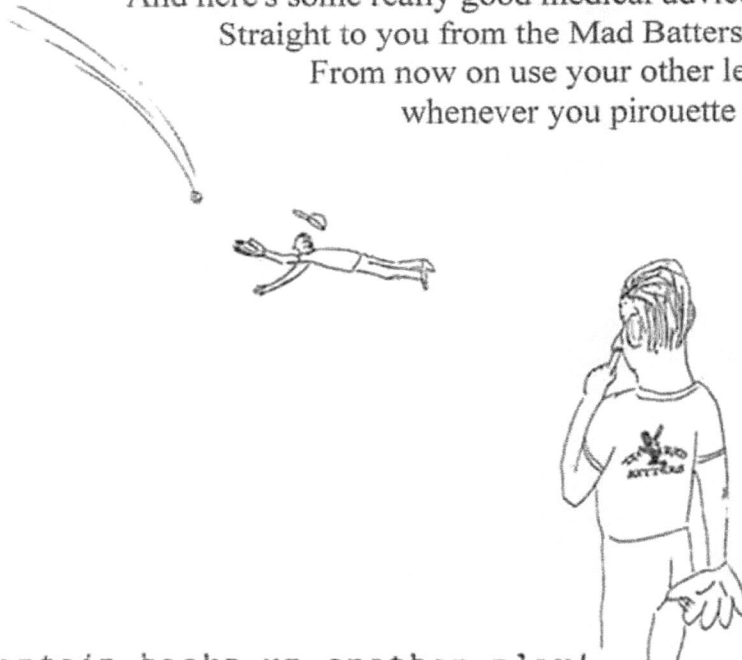

Team Captain backs up another play!

FANTASTIC FINAL GAME TEAM

Well with the last bugs having been tracked down and corrected in the Mad Batters' Computer Optimized Strategy & Tactics (COMPOST) software, we finally got it together: In a hotly contested fun game both our Stealth Offense and our Stealth Defense worked to perfection, giving us a convincing 7 – 18 loss to F.O.R.D. and earning us not only 3rd Place in C-3 League and 33rd of 36 overall, but also – as BobC put it so delicately – *"Total mediocrity in the lowest league!?!"*.

The pitching staff was never more accurate, managing to hit each F.O.R.D. in the bat several times apiece. The rest of the defense performed almost brilliantly, determined to cover up for errors at first base. (Just kidding, Bones !) Chris's hand-puppet/pot-holder glove missed a hit to 3rd base in the 3rd inning, and instead the ball just hit her in the pot, so to speak; ouch!

Well if our pitching was deadly accurate and our defense was almost sensational, what can we say about our offense? Okay, but what else? Every Mad Batter got to first base at least once this time. In fact June and Wiley got to first, second and/or third base about three times each within one minute of classic C-3 League suspense and action! With one away in the 4th inning, June was on first and Wiley was on second when Team Captain drilled this enormous pop-up to the F.O.R.D. shortstop. Since our crack staff of base coaches had clearly warned both runners to tag up if it was a flyball, June & Wiley both came back to their bags the minute the ball was hit and then proceeded at their usual blazing speed toward 2nd & 3rd, respectively. Unfortunately "tag up" means "after the ball is caught" and not "after the ball is hit" – these subtle distinctions are really inappropriate for C-3 League – so now June & Wiley had become fair game! Well what with all the base coaching and confusion, our two almost-fastest base runners proceeded to dash back and forth between bases 1, 2 and 3 like ducks in a shooting gallery. When the dust finally cleared, F.O.R.D. had logged 6 outs: 1 fly out, 2 throws to the bag and 3 tags on the baseline. The umpire had to call a 15 minute timeout to regan his composure. Almost attagirl & -boy anyway June & Wiley; it's the thought that counts.

Post Game Attitude Adjustment at Chester Drawers was understandably wild and woolly. The Mules had lost to the Sidewinders who had thus secured First Place in C-3 League. Notwithstnding ballgame results, the Roach and I decided there should be a really meaningful playoff at Chester Drawers, for *"Life, the Universe and Everything"* as the Roach put it.

SO MANY PITCHES, SO LITTLE TIME

Here's to the Mad Batters of 1990: a really fantastic team!
Whose 1990 preseason potential fulfilled my wildest (softball) dream!
Alas a few runs slipped past the defense,
All our Grand Slams failed to reach the fence,
But what the heck, we're 33rd out of 36 …
…not as mediocre as it may seem!????!

HAPPY BIRTHDAY TO MS. X

Here's a birthday poem to Ms. X:
    I promise not to tell how old you are today!
        Besides, you look so incredibly young
            that nobody would believe me anyway.
You're classically beautiful, your hair is a crown,
    you dress in clothes that are elegant but bright:
        They suggest rather than cover a body that's stunning,
          whose vision keeps men awake all night.
Yet there's more than just beauty: you're a fascinating person as well
    with a mind that's quick and witty and smart.
        You're nobody's bimbo nor coldly liberated either;
         you're a mixture of logic, intuition and heart.
I'm delighted to be your friend; you're thoughtful and fun,
    and naturally I'm in love and in lust with you too.
        But of course every other man feels the same way toward you as I
         -- and of course you already knew.
So don't get alarmed that I put it in writing
    (perhaps I should have been more cautious);
        I only did it to wish you a Very Happy Birthday
         -- I hope this poem doesn't make you nauseous!

        or

HOT DAMN !!

Here's to ladies over forty
    from a man who's somewhat older:
        You're not only more beautiful than ever,
      but you're wiser
          and a helluva lot bolder!

YUPPIE BLUES

Once there was a yuppie who grew older every day.
Not just linearly but *exponentially* her time sped away.
When she turned 32
She was feeling so blue
That she filled her entire Jacuzzi with Oil of Ole.

HAPPY BIRTHDAY LADY !!!

This poem's a little late,
and your birthday is now just history;
And since I want to remain your friend,
Herein your new age remains a mystery!
I hope you enjoyed your special day
And reflected on all the time that's passed away
And plan to enjoy to the fullest your remaining years
-- of which there's now one less to be!

ANOTHER GOOD DEED GONE WRONG

Larry's fifty, and he's never looked better!
(Oops! that's both the good news and bad;
my face couldn't be redder!)
A half century plus nine months ago
His mother passed up a chance to say, "NO !"
And now we're stuck with the world's oldest bed wetter !!

PERIODIC POETRY

Periodically Patricia stayed abed,
during which periods she really saw red!
Her friends wanted so
to help stem the flow
That one even suggested using
a loaf of Wonder Bread!?!

MOVING POETRY

Once upon a time there was a damsel in distress:
  Requested moving muscle to help change her address
   And I sincerely wanted to help this friend
    to relieve her of some stress.
Alas, her plan conflicted with an earlier one of mine
  To take other friends sailing out o'er the salty brine,
   And of course, the lady smiled bravely and said,
    "That's okay; everything will be fine."
With dock lines in hand on the appointed day at dawn,
  After a restless night I stifled a yawn;
   A moment's guilt -- then we were gone.
The sea was calm; the air was clear;
  The horizons were far -- but my conscience was near,
   And the crew was puzzled that I drank so much beer.
We moored at Catalina; we swam; we ate;
  We rowed and hiked and played until the hour was late,
   ... And as I fell asleep I wondered about the lady's fate?
I envisioned this giant desk -- her arms and legs sticking out beneath it --
  All the way down at the bottom of the stairs where they had lit,
   And heard her very frustrated voice saying, "*Awshit!*"
Next day my mood was better, and I was feeling a lot more glib.
  After all, "This boat's for escape!", I thought to myself as I hoisted the jib,
   And besides, think what a helluva nice letter
    I'm going to receive from Women's Lib!!

CREW BLUE

Here's to the crew: they're almost always late!
  The appointed hour comes and goes,
   but I'm still waiting at the gate.
Tho' I invited twenty -- hoping somehow to maybe see ten --
  Only two showed up ...
   ... *Surprise, Surprise*: the skipper's frustrated again!
But I've grown philosophical:
  Tho' a skipper's life can be maddening and hard,
   Sitting at the dock waiting for crew
    sure as hell beats working in the yard!!

SHIPSHAPE !!!
To the vessel *Laurie D*
     and to her skipper and namesake / crew:
          The skipper of the *Dave-y-Joan's* sends his greetings;
               it's a pleasure sharing a slip with you.
Making it into my slip without hitting your boat
     is my priority navigational goal,
          But please be advised that whenever Laurie's on deck
               my vessel's essentially out of control.
Her beauty's so gorgeous and stunning
     that every crewman becomes a fool,
          And if -- oh please! -- she's wearing a bikini
               my deck's disgustingly awash with drool.
With tongues hanging down and eyes bugging out
     crew rushes starboard to better take stock
          And 9 times out of 10 even *I* get distracted
               and wind up hitting the dock.
So next time you see us coming into port
     please lock her in the vault,
          'Cause any property damage and/or broken hearts
               are otherwise all Laurie's fault!

GOT XMAS ?

MAD OR MERRY: WHAT'S THE DIFFERENCE?

Merry Christmas from your team captain;
    here's wishing you and your family and friends
        My very best for your well being:
            may the coming year be filled with bliss that never ends!
May all of your wildest dreams come true;
    may the obstacles to your success move aside so you can pass;
        And may your automobiles need nary a single repair,
            nor tires nor oil nor gas.
But if misfortune should somehow befall you
    -- like getting locked overnight
        with your millions of dollars in the family vault --
          Please remember that I'm the one
            who wished you only good things;
              All the bad shit is somebody else's fault !!

December 1997

Merry Christmas from Judy & Dave in Florida
    and Happy New Year too !!
        We hope this finds you well and happy
            … and the stock market didn't make you blue?

We love our new home at Burnt Store Marina
    -- we're 10 miles from the nearest stop light !
        The people are great, the weather's fantastic,
            and mosquito-spray DC-3's are a sight !

Of hurricane threats there was nary a one
    -- ironically California ducked two !?! --
        but we did have three 'gators ('tho rather small)
            which were relocated to some lucky zoo.

We thoroughly enjoyed all 38 visitors
    -- *The Tour* has become really nice.
        The highlight (of course) is boating thru Charlotte Harbor,
            and we only ran aground once or thrice.

Tho' 10 miles by 30, the harbor averages 10 feet deep
    so a skipper is wise to be cautious ….
        …. Merry Christmas again. I've got to stop now:
            this poem's starting to make me nauseous !

December 2005

It's December already, and I'm running out of time.
    So my standards will be even lower
        for this year's little rhyme.

Christmas came upon us so swift it was amazing.
    I wish it was still summer
        with sunshine all ablazing.

Instead the temp is dropping -- I may need a big snow blower !?!
    (Like I said: this year poetry standards
        are significantly lower.)

It's going to be a cold one -- yesterday one of the golfers wore a sweater ! --
    and there are other signs
        it's gonna get worse before it gets any better.

Icicle lights are drooping from the Spanish red tile roofs
    (it's a wonder they don't break
        under all the reindeers' hoofs.)

And on my walk to Starbucks it was plain for all to see
    that it had snowed on one of the neighbor's lawn
        in the outline of a Christmas tree !?!

But what the heck, we're mostly indoors and happy as can be
    with AOL and Photoshop
        all running on Windows XP.

Did I mention I was rushing this poem, and I've still got stamps to stick?
    Merry Christmas and Happy New Year !!!
        (I hope it didn't make you sick.)

Merry Christmas from our family to yours:
    Wishing you all Health & Happiness in the New Year !

December 2006

The Christmas Season is now upon us; 2006 is racing to an end.
　　　It's time to stop and count our blessings,
　　　　　　thinking of family and every friend.

(This year's poem was started early, providing time for eloquence and class.
　　　Not like last year's which was rushed and hurried
　　　　　　and was mostly just pulled from my ass.)

We cruised up the Rhine at a leisurely pace (you could barely hear the wake's hiss)
　　　ending up in Lucerne to relax and unwind
　　　　　　and eat chocolates as made by the Swiss.

Of course we don't normally indulge like that: I mostly eat twigs and dirt,
　　　and I exercise almost daily it seems
　　　　　　unless something comes up or I hurt.

Janet and Mickey enjoy a cabin in Big Bear, Leo thinks WVA is terrific,
　　　Robert turned 40, Terry does Mud Runs,
　　　　　　and Julie sailed across the Pacific.

If our social life seemed reclusive this year -- some may have thought me dead --
　　　it's only because I was overwhelmed
　　　　　　with projects such as *The Bed*:

Started in early spring, made of wood, 'twas delivered in early winter,
　　　and "sleeps" pretty good, according to our friend,
　　　　　　except for an occasional splinter.

Did I mention the "Master Suite" remodel?　This project is still underway;
　　　A whole new look will be completed and done
　　　　　　before Santa comes Christmas Day.

Meanwhile Best Wishes from San Clemente
　　　(not far from the San Onofre nuke);
　　　　　　May 2007 be your best year ever !
　　　　　　　　　… and may this poetry not make you puke !?!

Merry Christmas from our family to yours:
　　　Wishing you all Health & Happiness in the New Year !

43

December 2008

Again this year I'm running late
    (… which sums up my entire '08 !)
        So much to do, so little time,
            And now I'm stumped by this darn rhyme!

Hence this holiday you'll get off easy:
    My poem's too short
        To make you queasy !?!

December 2009

Why can't I ever seem to remember
    To start this rhyme before early December?!?
        … Causing sleepless nights and lots of stress
            And excessive use of my margarita blender !

On the other hand -- tho' it's oddly perverse --
    I cherish the time it takes to write this verse,
        Reflecting on family and friends (here and gone)
            With fond memories that warm my universe.

Was that last line poetic license abuse?
    Was a reference to the universe too obtuse?
        Hey: get over it, it'll probably just get worse;
            For example, my candidate never shot a moose !

But I digress; 'tis time to be of good cheer,
    This merry holiday time of year
        When our very best wishes go out to you:
            All our family and friends, both far and near.

December 2010

A decade into century twenty-one
    It's fair to ask, "Are we still having fun?"
        The answer of course ambiguous:
        'Tho the year's been fairly big for us
It's already December but this poem's just begun !?!

Fortunately the fotos that surround
    Tell our yearlong story without a sound
        And yet to many eyes they scream,
        "Hey look: check out that awesome scene !"
….. Or at least, "Hey look: Dave's gained another pound !"

Merry Christmas from our family to yours:
    Wishing you all Health & Happiness in the New Year !

December 2011

I started writing in January this year
    To "*en-poem*" deep thoughts I'd remember,
        But I dove so deep that when I awoke
            -- Oh damn! -- It was early December!?!

Nevertheless, there's plenty of time
    To pen something truly and utterly profound;
        And here it comes now …
            …. No wait, that was gas;
                What a rude and disgusting sound!

Two-thousand-eleven was a wonderful year:
    We joined Judy's cousin for a cruise down the Rhone,
        … And a couple of months later we adopted a dog … !??!
        Now we can hardly leave *Gizmo* alone !

He's totally sweet, he barks almost never,
    We love watching him at play or at rest …
        … Plus we're reluctant to let him out of sight indoors
            'cause his "toilet" habits are uncertain at best.

But I'm sure we'll outsmart him -- 'tho *when* is unclear --
    And he'll stop chewing on everything pretty …
        Then someday in the future we'll get a full night's sleep …

    OMG: HE JUST ATE HALF THIS DITTY!!!

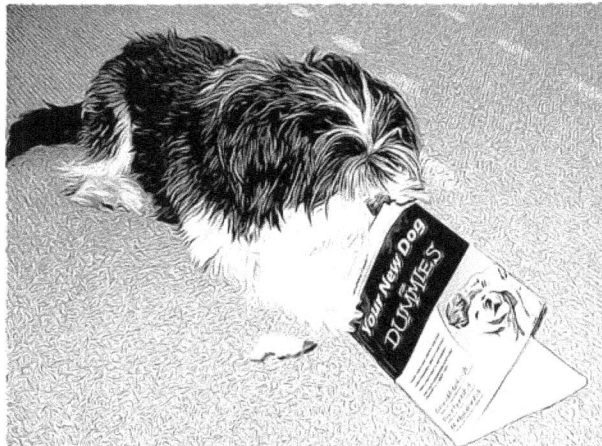

December 2012

In 2012, the Mayan Calendar said,
      by December 21 we'd all be dead.
           So: to start this poem or procrastinate?
           The latter of course,
               .... and now it's too late;
Thus you'll just have to suffer all these fotos instead !?!

****

December 2013... !?!

The first draft of this poem was deemed *Bizarre!!* by those who edit;
      It was suggested I retrieve each copy, take it to the garage and shred it !
          "But *The Voices in my head* ...," I pleaded
              -- real sincere and with obvious piety --
                  ... Met with icy stares and veiled invitations
                  to join the Dead Poets Society.

So now I'm back at square number one,
      and I've missed my poetic deadline.
          There's a very good chance I'll have to work late,
             staying up way past my bedtime. ...
... (Or not ?) ... '13 was yet another amazing year gone by;
          Tho' with some lows, overall our year was mostly high:
             Enjoying family and friends we love, plus some travel too,
               As shown in all these fotos *all*
                  -- Our very best wishes to ~~most~~ of you !!!

December 2017

Why can't I ever seem to remember
    To start this rhyme before early December?!?
        … Causing sleepless nights and lots of stress
            and excessive use of my margarita blender !

On the other hand – tho' it's oddly perverse –
    I cherish the time to write this verse,
        Reflecting on family and friends (here and gone)
            with fond memories that warm my universe.

Judy's star, more than a year in the sky,
    shines brightly as ever in memory's eye.
        She'd be pleased how I accomplish our domestic chores
            … except caring for houseplants, which tend to die.

But I digress: 'tis time to be of good cheer,
    this merry holiday time of year
        When my very best wishes go out to you:
            All our family and friends, both far and near.

    Merry Christmas from our family to yours.
        Wishing you all Health and Happiness
        in the New Year !!

December 2019

The holiday season is fast upon us
    So Dave's composing a Christmas rhyme,
        Expressing in poem his fond regard for you all:
            Every neighbor, friend, family member of mine.

Alas, until the last minute he waited
    So as usual this poem's pretty rough.
        For example he matched words "*rhyme*" and "*mine*"
          And tho' noted he thought, "*Close enough!?!*"

But moving on I'll close with this:
    I think you are truly first rate.
        May your Christmas be merry and 2020 the best;
          May good health and happiness be your fate!?!

Merry Christmas from our family to yours.
  Wishing you all Peace and Happiness in the New Year !!

Got 80 ???

ANCIENT HISTORY, Part 1

Here's to all my family and friends:
    Having *you* in my life means a lot to me.
        I've ridden this planet 80 trips 'round the sun
            (How many more are to come is life's mystery).

Thanks to you, I've enjoyed almost every day,
    So I wish *you* all happiness, come what may.
        Please enjoy to the fullest your remaining years
            – of which there's now one less to be.

T + 4,560,000,080 and Counting

80 trips around the sun
    is all that Dave has got.
        To many people younger than me
            That seems like an awful lot !?!
But in perspective,
    before Dave's 80
        Earth had almost 5 **Billion** to show,
And while Dave's got maybe 5, 10 or 20,
    Earth's got another 5 **Billion** revs to go !!!!

ANCIENT HISTORY, Part 2

Wonderful people are born in January
    when the weather is really cold.
        (Or at least that was true many years ago
            -- this birthday boy's really old!)
His age is LXXX (four score) years –
    That's ancient and truly Amazing !
        We're talking at least a four alarm fire
            if the fire marshal spots all his candles blazing!
So treat him nice: not just because he's old
    and losing all of his hair,
        But rather because -- if your luck holds out too --
            you'll need a friend familiar with Medicare.

ENJOYING IRRELEVANCE   or   NOT QUITE DEAD YET

I am truly ancient;
      since Judy died I live alone,
            But my "children" live nearby
                  so now and then I see them
                        or now and then we talk on the phone.

My stepson and his family
      are a nearby source of joy as well,
            As is his older brother living in West Virginia
                  and apparently doing swell.

Along with everybody else
      this virus has me trapped indoors,
            So I take more naps than usual,
                but while I lie here
                      my brain really roars.

I'm remembering all the things from my past --
      at my age that's a huge amount –
            And I've stored many questions and points of view …
                … that nobody seems to want.

Of course I know that's how life goes,
      when I was younger I didn't give a shit,
            and only pretended to be listening
                while my elders babbled on
                    like they'd never quit!?!

So now I just stand on the sidelines,
      watching problems gain ground
            like a herd of *elephants*,
                But at least I've managed to write a rhyme
                  making light of my new *irrelevance*!??!

GOT MILK?
Medical scientists are generally assholes;
      for job security making up mysterious Latin words,
          But their latest research is so amazing[++]
             that I'm giving high praise to those incredible nerds!?!
They've sorta discovered the way aging works,
      and maybe a path to longer life,
          But as usual their explanation is so complex
             that you've thought to slit the speaker's throat with a knife.
I'll try to explain in everyday English
      using words that you learned in first grade,
          and tho' a bit long, the lesson's not painful;
             Just pay attention, don't be afraid.
At the molecular level males and females are the same,*
      our bodies are made of billions of cooties.
          (*Except that the males like jokes about farts --
             what your mother quaintly called "*tooties*").
A cootie, you see, is like a little sausage,
      a strand of *fusilli** attached like a horse's mane …
          (*Pasta makers are also assholes: when they mangle spaghetti
             they give the result a mysterious Latin name.)
… But I digress; metaphorically the sausage part feeds on the strand of *fusilli*
      which becomes shorter with every bite,
          And tho' it normally takes many years to consume
             when that finally happens, it's "*Turn out the light*!?!"
When eventually all of your cooties die,
      concurrently you take your last breath.
          So the secret to longer life is to put your cooties on a diet
             so they eat more slowly but don't starve to death.
The way to achieve that, the medical scientists found, was to
      "Drink milk just *one percent* lowfat --
          If it's more than *one*, your cooties eat faster,
             and you know the unhappy outcome of that!?! "
If they'd stopped right there, we'd breathe a sigh of relief,
      knowing the key to life everlasting…
          "…By the way," they continued, "drinking *NO* milk's as bad,
             casting doubt on that one percent finding."
Did I mention medical scientists are generally assholes,
      for job security drawing conclusions inconclusive!?!
          "We're almost there, give us one more Grant,
             and by next year we'll be just as elusive!?!"

[++] https://news.byu.edu/intellect/drinking-1-milk-instead-of-2-milk-accounts-for-4-5-years-of-less-aging-in-adults   Drinking low-fat milk is associated with longer telomeres in adults

MOMS
&
DADS

Happy Mother's Day !!!
Here's to every lady who's a Mother
    Without you there'd be neither
        a sister nor a brother.
It's incredible you have/had
    a baby-making factory in your uterus
        What a fascinating way to make
            people who are new to us.
But as you know,
    the miracle of birth is just the start
        Followed by years & years & years & years
            of Mothering with all your heart.
Watching a child learn and develop
    is truly a joy to be seen;
        Tho' "joy" has different definitions
            when he or she becomes a teen!
No matter, Moms are always there
    every step along the way,
        And tho' we celebrate you formally
            on just this special day,
You're always in our heart and soul;
    we can never thank you enough …
        …. Okay, I've got to stop now,
            this poem's making my stomach
                feel pretty rough!?!

Happy Father's Day !!!
Here's to Men:
    we just stick it in,
        And thereafter
            we just play with the kid !?!
If we've done it right
    they turn out bright,
        So we just do it again and again !!

4 POEMS TOO FAR?

A Poem Too Far?
      or
      Can I Be In *The Dead Poet's Society* Now?

I started writing this years ago   (12-10-10)
    to "*en-poem*" deep thoughts I remember,
        But I dove so deep that when I awoke
            my ashes were just an ember!?!
When I began
    there was plenty of time
        to pen something truly and utterly profound;
            And here it comes now …
                …. No wait, that was gas;
                    What a rude and disgusting sound!
Two-thousand-TBD was a wonderful year,
      …… except for the part where I die …….
        But it's been a great ride,
            and I'm probably glad it's over
                … give me another year and I'll try to think why.
I'd planned to live forever,
    I mostly ate twigs and dirt,
        And I exercised almost daily it seemed
            unless something came up or I hurt.
But apparently we *die* sooner or later …
    … and of course I was hoping for later!
        So I guess it's Plan C: ashes scattered on the ocean,
            soul riding *Up* in that Gold Elevator?
You know: you get old, your dick stops workin',
    and many other best friends are dead;
        So life's not as fun, the lust and laughter are subdued …
            … You think, "Why bother to get out of bed?"
I'll tell you why: it's the *Lady* on my right
    and the *Friends* and *Family* who I cherish
        … Plus I feel a little guilty about all my stuff in the garage
            that they'll have to sort thru after I perish

And there's still a bunch to laugh at
　　　-- tho' it's often gallows humor --
　　　　　this one always tickles me to the max:
　　　　　　　A **loudly proclaimed** high frequency theory
　　　　　　　　　... woven thru *low* frequency facts !?!
Did I mention our brains *love* to speculate,
　　　drawing conclusions usually optimistic?
　　　　　Yet we're always surprised
　　　　　　　when our schedules and costs
　　　　　　　　　are usually unrealistic!?!
Oops: I've digressed -- swerved wildly off course --
　　　this poem was meant to be brief,
　　　　　'Twas meant to convey **my fondest regards for you all**;
　　　　　　　may joy and mirth follow this, not grief !?!
I sincerely wish you all health and happiness;
　　　may obstacles to your success move aside so you can pass,
　　　　　And may your automobiles need nary a single repair
　　　　　　　nor tires nor oil nor gas !?!
But if misfortune should somehow befall you
　　　-- like getting locked overnight
　　　　　with your millions of dollars in the family vault --
　　　　　　　Please remember I'm the one
　　　　　　　　　who wished you only good things;
　　　　　　　　　　　All the bad shit is somebody else's fault !!
And yes I know I've plagiarized
　　　from my other dittys,
　　　　　the better to complete this rhyme,
　　　　　　　But it saved me quite a lot of
　　　　　　　　　what I don't have any more of:
　　　　　　　　　　　All together now: can you say, "*Time*!?!"

A(nother) Final Poem

Another final poem from Dave
　　　whose ashes were tossed upon the ocean:
　　　　　Hopefully you didn't toss your lunch too
　　　　　　　because of the constantly heaving wave motion !??!

Got Nap?

Here's gallows humor that's really deep:
    Take naps to improve odds
        that you'll die in your sleep !?!

Last Call *

This is to report my fatal illness --
    I couldn't be any sicker --
        I've been wondering what was going to kill me,
            but I was hoping for something quicker!?!

Instead it's fucking cancer,
    eating me away from deep inside;
        So instead of a lightning-fast heart attack
        I'm in for a long painful slide.

Because I'm ancient I don't plan to fight it;
    I'll join hospice, thus being at home when I die.
    So this is likely my last smart-ass poem;
    I'm writing to say, *"Goodbye" !?!*

---

* *Still just kidding; no sign of cancer or heart disease so far (2023) !?!*

At No Extra Charge ...

10-22-88 *Rocket Lobster*: Dave + Larry + Dan + Dayna. Spent a weekend in Emerald Bay for opening of lobster season. The boys came up with a very sizeable lobster which we determined to boil and eat that very night (although I had prepared my special canned spaghetti just in case). Having procured a pretty large pot for that event, I soon had it full of water in a rolling boil. Larry, the only one who had previously seen a lobster cooked, warned Dan to stand away from the water which might "splash a bit." Upon being dropped (tail first) into the boiling water "Charlie" launched himself 20 feet into the sky, but fortunately landed back on the deck of the galley DOA. He was delicious after a bit more time in the pot. *Charlie's Karma*? Mr. Motor failed as we departed for home Sunday afternoon, so in the usual very light air, Larry expertly managed to get us back to Long Beach 18.5 hours later, with Dan doing a bit of paddling (a technique to be used again) and a final tow to the dock by a passing stinkpot. Any of 'em you can walk away from was a good one????????

2001 *We got owls, part 1*: When Judy & I had first toured our cul de sac in PGI we'd noticed some small burrowing owls across street under neighbors' curbside culvert. (Neighbors had named them *Oscar* and *Olivia*.) Neighbors explained that these owls were territorial and seemed to nest every year on the street but at different sites. In '01 it was our turn: they burrowed a nest right outside our front window. At first we thought it rather cute: mother appeared rarely, but father sat guard on ledge above front window ... shitting! It was illegal to disturb nest during nesting season, so we tolerated them. Eventually -- at Kay & Clark's expense -- we discovered that tho' father would screech & spread wings menacingly, he would not actually attack a visitor. After nesting season we took pains to remove the nest, and they did indeed move on. P.S. We never observed any baby owls.

5-13-02 *We got owls, part 2*: Owls *Oscar* & *Olivia* had chosen to nest in culvert at corner of our cul de sac (Bobwhite) and main drag (Whippoorwill). One day we were pleasantly surprised to note a tiny white baby owl was with them. Of course I rushed to grab my camera, and Judy and I went out there to marvel. For some reason the baby decided it was *imperative* to climb over blacktop lip-o-road (as high as baby-o itself) and cross to the other side. A cliché moment? This obviously concerned *O & O*, but they were unable to stop baby-o. Judy and I actually took up stations to stop traffic so baby-o could successfully cross. Just as baby-o began to totter across, a large raven appeared above with two red-wing blackbirds in hot pursuit. Spotting baby-o the raven dove down (in tight formation with his pursuers), but at the last minute papa *Oscar* sprang into the air and intercepted the raven. For a moment the airspace was filled with all four birds, and then the raven-and-his-escorts pulled up and seemed to head away. Whereupon *Oscar* returned to his guard station at road's edge ... whereupon (in a shorter span of time than it takes to read all this) the raven-and-his-escorts made an amazing diving U-turn, and the raven scooped baby-o up in his beek and flew off, the red-wing blackbirds still right on his tail. Judy and I were totally stunned as were *Oscar* and *Olivia* who could not figure out where baby-o had gone. We may now understand why we never saw any baby burrowing owls and indeed maybe why their species is threatened!?!

62

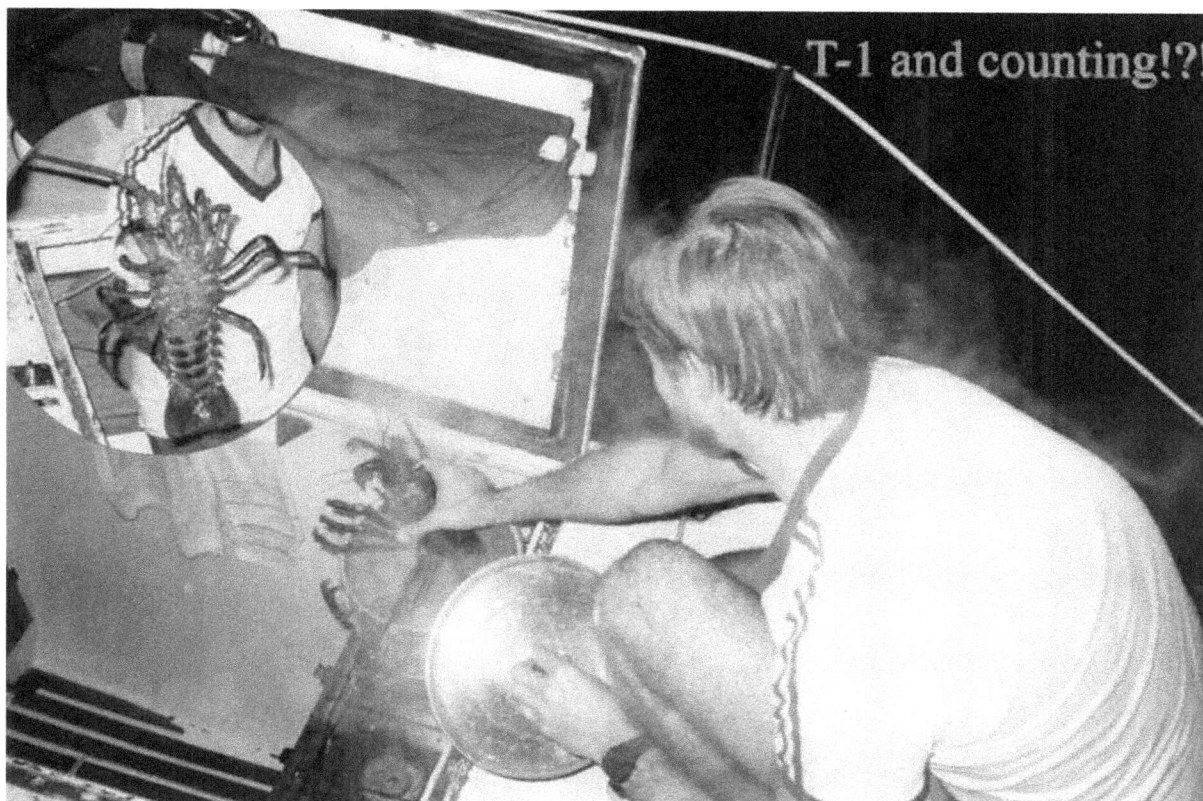

T-1 and counting!?!

Rocket Lobster ⬆

⬇Got Owls?

Why did the
baby owl (almost)
cross the road??

Dad standing guard
.... almost